HEART OF A DOG

Heart of a Dog

A satirical tragicomedy
in one act
for solo actor

by Robert Astle and Agnès Limbos

© 1994, Robert Astle and Agnès Limbos

Adapted from the novella of the same name by Mikhail Bulgakov, translated by Mirra Ginsburg, Grove Press, New York.

All rights reserved. No part of this book may be reproduced, for any reason, by any means, without permission of the publisher. This play is fully protected under copyright law of Canada and all other countries of the Copyright Union and is subject to royalty. Changes to the script are expressly forbidden without written consent of the authors. Rights to produce, film, record in whole or in part, in any medium or in any language, by any group, amateur or professional, are retained by the authors. All production inquiries should be directed to: Nuage Editions, P.O. Box 8, Station E, Montreal, Quebec, H2T 3A5

The authors wish to thank the following agencies for their generous support: The Canada Council, Alberta Foundation for the Arts, Small Change Theatre, Commissariat général aux Relations internationales de la Communauté Française de Belgique.

The authors would like to acknowledge the following people for their inspiration and support for this work: Marina Popova, Alex Nadezhdhin, Mirra Ginsburg, Trish Barclay, Françoise Bloch, Marie-Katelin Rutten, Billy Merwick, Daniel Meillieur, Jan Miller, Jan Henderson, Jan Stirling, Carine Ermans, and Marc Elst, and William and Dorothy Astle. Also thanks to Lynda Clark, Full Grown Productions, Daniel Daniel, Luc d'Haegeleer, Helen Wong, Grove Press Inc., Jean Seydel and Ellen Pierce.

Cover artwork by Daniel Daniel.
Cover design by Ramez Rabbat.
Photography by Luc d'Haegeleer.

Printed and bound in Canada by Imprimerie d'Edition Marquis Ltée.
Published with the assistance of The Canada Council.
Dépôt légal, Bibliotheque national du Québec and the National Library of Canada.

Canadian Cataloguing in Publication Data

Astle, Robert
    Heart of a dog

(Performance series)
ISBN 0-921833-03-2

    I. Limbos, Agnès   II. Title   III. Series

PS8551.S875H43 1994   C812'.54   C94-900790-0
PR9199.3.A88H43 1994

NuAge Editions, P.O. Box 8, Station E, Montréal, Québec, H2T 3A5

Dedicated to all the stray mongrels of Moscow

PRODUCTION NOTES

Actor: Robert Astle
Director: Agnès Limbos
Machines/visuals: Didier Caffonnette

1990 Creation:
           Rhode St. Genese, Belgium
           Preview performances

1991 Performance:
           High Performance Rodeo, Calgary, Alberta
           Edmonton Fringe Theatre Festival

1992 Canadian Tour:
           Poor Alex Theatre, Toronto, Ontario
           Kaasa Theatre, Edmonton, Alberta
           Yukon Arts Centre, Whitehorse, Yukon

1993 UK Tour:
           West Yorkshire Playhouse, Leeds
           Traverse Theatre, Edinburgh
           Tron Theatre, Glasgow
           Battersea Arts Centre, London

1994 USA Tour:
           Lebanon Valley College, Pennsylvania
           Theatre of Creation Festival
           Lehigh University, Bethlehem, Pennsylvania

Reading Notes

Character: **Polygraph Polygraphovich Sharikov**

Polygraph is a grotesque character, half-man, half-dog. He is vulgar and stocky. His face is covered in dirt; his hands, filthy and paw-like, jut out of a long, ratty, plum-coloured smoking jacket. He wears a repulsive red tie, a poisonously ugly shirt, torn brown pants, and scuffed patent leather shoes. On his head he wears a Russian-style fake fur hat, the flaps pulled down over his ears, topped off with welder's goggles. He also wears a small fat suit around his belly, knee pads, and a mouth mask made of cheese cloth or other soft, absorbent material stuffed into his upper lip.

Polygraph speaks with a Russian/Eastern European accent. He is a rough-hewn raconteur who addresses the public directly, narrating his stories using flashback and storytelling. The public is the "witness" to the terrible events he describes.

Polygraph also plays the rest of the cast of ironic characters. When he imitates the voice and physicality of these characters, this is indicated in the text by "Doctor," "Girl," "Gossip," and "Guest."

All the playing zones indicated in the script are imaginary—"office," "street," "apartment," "hallway." When Polygraph goes into the "office" he is in fact merely walking into the "office area" which is sharply delineated by a square clearly defined on the floor cloth by sharp focus lights downstage right. All the action is played on a 14' x 12' raw canvas floor cloth. This cloth represents Polygraph's 16 square arshin (approximately 12 square yards). There is no formal set except for Polygraph's two large suitcases, and a carpet bag which is strapped to one of the suitcases. Polygraph's samovar is packed into the carpet bag. The suitcases contain all the props used in the dream installations. It all looks hastily put together.

All imaginary props are indicated with quotation marks (e.g. "sausage").

"He is dangerous."

Scene 1. Thrown Out

>*The lights come up on a raw canvas floor cloth on an empty stage.*
>
>*Silence.*
>
>*The lights darken, then gradually brighten to make shadows.*
>
>*Polygraph explodes onto the stage from upstage right. A cigarette dangles from his filthy mouth. He has been thrown out of the apartment with his two suitcases. He trips, losing a shoe, and skids to a halt on his belly. He slowly pulls himself together, and looks directly at the audience. He points back in the direction from which he has come.*

Polygraph: He is dangerous.

>*(Muttering under his breath.)* Bastard, son of a bitch, he threw me on to the street. *(He takes his cigarette out of his mouth.)* Look at that… That bastard ripped my jacket.

Arooo ooooo

>*Rising, Polygraph points upstage right.*

He is dangerous.

>*Muttering, he scratches his face and straightens his tie.*

I don't believe it. I will get my justice. Son of a bitch, bastard.

Arooo ooo

>*Polygraph sniffs the air, catching a familiar scent. He spots his shoe, sniffs it and snatches it up possessively.*

This is mine.

>*He puts the shoe on, while muttering oaths in the upstage right direction of the "Doctor." He points at his shoes.*

These are patent leather.

Suddenly he notices the toppled suitcases.

My things!

Polygraph grabs the suitcases and takes a few steps. He stops. He takes a few more steps. He stops. He takes a few more steps. He looks all over the stage. It is obvious that he is lost.

He howls.

Arooooooooooo

He speaks intimately to the audience.

I don't know where to go.

Polygraph sniffs the air, then paws the ground with his feet. He puts down his suitcases triumphantly and proclaims:

This is *my* sixteen square arshin, and here I *stay*.

The lights snap to full brightness.

Polygraph strikes a ludicrously proud pose, his nose in the air. He jams his cigarette into his mouth.

Bastard, son of bitch, I will get my justice. Look at that… Bastard, threw me into the street like that. And look at that. He ripped my jacket.

Aroooo

A shard of a memory stabs Polygraph.

"Doctor": Sit…

Polygraph: —He used to say.

Polygraph simply sits on a suitcase, and points out that he can be a good dog.

You see? I'm sitting.

"Doctor": STAY...

> *Polygraph obediently crosses his arms.*

Polygraph: You see? I'm staying.

"Doctor": SPEAK...

> *Polygraph casts about for words.*

Polygraph: I don't know what to say...

> *In a rough, arrogant voice he begins speaking directly to individual members of the audience.*

Hey you, give me a smoke or I give you a poke.

Hey you, back of the bus... Evening paper.

> *His voice softens.*

Hey you, little apple.

> *He speaks proudly.*

You see? I'm speaking.

"You see these teeth? When I am angry I go like that."

Scene 2. The Girl (Flashback)

Polygraph leaps to his feet downstage centre.

He speaks directly and confidentially to the audience.

Polygraph: You would not believe what *he* did to me.

I had a girl. I met her. I said to her—

He dashes upstage left, poses suggestively, straightens his ugly tie, tugs at his torn pants, and shines his scuffed shoes on the back of his pant legs.

Hey you, little apple.

She was beautiful…

He sees the "girl" approaching stage left.

Red ribbon in her hair, green eyes, black dress, high heeled shoes. I said to her—

He speaks sincerely, honestly.

I'm a good man. I have a good psyche. It's just cats I hate.

He takes the "girl's" arm, and they stroll, arm in arm, across the floor cloth.

She likes me…we are walking…we are talking.

(To "girl.") Beautiful day, unh?

"Girl": Replies in Russian-sounding gibberish.

Polygraph: I translate: "Very beautiful day."

She wants to see my apartment.

Polygraph shows her the "apartment."

I show her the lamp with the beautiful pink lampshade, and the things that go tinkling, tinkling, tinkling. I can tell by her green eyes that she is impressed by my apartment.

Pause...Polygraph stiffens.

Then that bastard, he comes in... First he looks up me and then down me, and then up her and down her.

"Doctor": And who, may I ask, is this?

Polygraph: I say: She is a typist. She will...

Polygraph mockingly crosses his arms.

...stay...with me.

"Doctor": Step into my office.

Polygraph: Not to me. To her... She follows...

Polygraph races after her to the "office area" downstage right. He stops at the "door."

I'm scratching.

Polygraph scratches.

I'm howling.

Aroooo...

Polygraph tries to open the "office door."

I'm locked outside.

He speaks directly to the audience.

You see what that bastard can do?

He spits vehemently in the direction of the "Doctor."

Then I hear something.

Lifting the ear flaps on his hat, he proudly shows his ears to audience.

You see these ears? These are very good ears for hearing.

He cocks an ear and listens to the conversation in the "office."

All I can hear is crying, crying, crying.

"Girl" : *(Her tone disbelieving and outraged.)* Speaks in Russian-sounding gibberish.

Polygraph: I translate: "You mean it was him? The one in the gateway? I think I will poison myself!"

Then I hear:

"Doctor": Here is twenty-five chervontsy. You'd better stay away from him. He is no good for nothing.

Polygraph speaks directly to the audience.

You see what that bastard did to me?

Polygraph looks toward the "office door" and sees the "girl."

She comes out. Her green eyes have changed. They are not going tinkling, tinkling, tinkling anymore. Then she spits... Just like this.

Polygraph crosses to the "office door." He momentarily takes on the physicality of the "girl." As the "girl," he looks disdainfully towards centre stage, then spits poisonously. Polygraph runs to centre stage to receive the "spit."

I see that spit coming towards me out of the corner of my eye. It is bitter, covered with lemon juice and blood. On each little gob, I can see knives and razor blades churning. It gets me right there.

He touches his cheek.

Arooooo-oooooo

Polygraph looks at the "spit" on his hand, then at the "office door." The "girl" is no longer there. He turns and sees her downstage left. He sprints to the edge of the floor cloth. He cocks his head, and poses like a dog watching her go, not at all understanding why…

All I can see is the back of her head.

He turns woefully to the audience.

She is gone.

Polygraph growls and gnashes his teeth ferociously. Bristling with rage, he stomps around the space. He stops suddenly and turns to audience.

You see these teeth?

He bares his teeth.

When I am angry, I go like that.

He points to his front teeth, making his "angry" teeth. He crosses to the upstage right entrance, looks offstage, and spits venomously in the direction of the "Doctor." He punches his cigarette angrily into his mouth.

She was beautiful. Green eyes…black dress…

Polygraph points upstage right and spits.

He is dangerous.

Polygraph howls to the rafters…

Arooooo-ooooo

Polygraph speaks intimately to the audience.

I don't know what to do.

He scratches pensively.

Perhaps…I move my suitcases.

Polygraph positions and repositions his suitcases as if he were arranging furniture. Finally, he sniffs the air, paws the ground, then proudly places them in their original positions.

Perhaps...I sit.

Polygraph sits down between the two suitcases.

You see, I'm sitting.

He mutters.

Bastard. Look at that. Threw me out into the street.

His anger increases.

Look at that. He ripped my jacket.

Growling and barking, Polygraph moves on all fours to the upstage right edge of the floor cloth toward the "Doctor."

Arroo aroo wooh wooh wooh.

He turns to the audience and points at his "angry" teeth.

Polygraph slinks back to the suitcases and furtively unpacks the carpet bag. He pulls out a little Indian rug, a Russian tea glass, and a water flask.

He mutters.

Mine.

He pulls the samovar out of the carpet bag.

Beautiful, hunh?

He places the tea glass on the lid of the samovar, and pours water into the glass from the water flask. He laps at the water...

Good water here, very good water.

"Then the rest of the water fell directly on his side."

Scene 3. The Story of a Cook, a Drop of Water and a Dog

> *Polygraph sits on stage right suitcase, and tests his tea water with a filthy finger. He decides it isn't hot enough and turns to look directly at the audience.*

Polygraph: I tell you a story...

> *The lights cross-fade to a warm intimate "storytelling" light focussed on the centre area.*

The story of a cook, a drop of water...and a dog. Now, once upon a time, there was a dog who lived in the city of Moscow...

> *He gestures at the samovar.*

Now, it was cold, snowing, winter...

> *Polygraph reaches into his pocket for some white confetti. He sprinkles it around the samovar, making the sound of a cold wind.*

Just like that. Now, have you ever been so cold that you cannot do that?

> *He tries to pry apart his frozen fingers.*

It was that cold. Now, that dog was starving. He had not eaten for two days. He saw a cafeteria across the street. He ran across the street. He scratched at the door...

> *He makes scratching sounds.*

Just like that... He howled...

Aroooo

Just like that. Now, the door opened. A warm wind blew out. He saw a pair of white pants...a cook. Now, that dog looked into the eyes of that cook...very nasty.

Now, that cook was holding a bucket full of hot water. He threw the hot water at that dog...

Polygraph gets to his feet in alarm.

The dog started to run, but his feet were slipping on the icy pavement. His paws, they started to bleed. Out of the corner of his eye, he saw a little drop of water coming straight towards him.

Polygraph watches the "water" come toward him.

It caught him right there.

He touches his cheek and lets out a surprised howl.

Arooooo

Just like that. Then the rest of the water fell directly on his side.

He howls in agony.

Aroo-aroo-aroo-ooooahhhhhh

Just like that. Now, that dog crawled along the icy pavement to a gateway. He howled.

Arooooo

A shaft of bright white light cuts across centre stage, Polygraph poses tragically, remembering the pain. He gazes up into the light. His voice is very fragile.

The blizzard roars a prayer for the dying, and I howl with it...

Arooooo-ooooo-ooooo

Ah people, people, a dog is hard to kill. His spirit clings to life.

Aroooo-oooooo.

Just like that.

> *Lights cross-fade to the intimate "storytelling" light.*

Now, that dog, he started to cry, but the tears couldn't even make it to the edge of his cheek. They froze right there, in the corner of his eye and he closed his eyes and he had a dream…

Just like this.

> *Polygraph makes wind sounds and tosses some confetti in the air. He walks into this little blizzard, and looks at the audience. The lights cross-fade to the cool blue "dream" light.*

Dream of the Park

Scene 4. Dream of the Park

Polygraph crosses to the smaller suitcase stage left. This suitcase has built-in, folding legs, which give elevation and improve sight lines. The interior of the suitcase lid is painted to look like a night sky and has small twinkling lights built in. All the props and dirt are bundled in the burlap pockets and folds of the suitcase.

The suitcase contains some dirt, small plastic trees, small white toy dogs, a dinner bell, a tattered umbrella, and a large red papier mâché bone. Other flotsam and jetsam in the dirt include a reflector, some tin cans, a red sock, a slipper, a cigarette package and a high heeled shoe.

Also in the dirt is Polygraph's evidence: a charred piece of a calendar, his work papers, a balled-up newspaper, a dog-eared blue book, and a small revolver.

Dream installation:

Polygraph makes the sound of the wind... He sets the suitcase up on its legs, then opens it, folds back the burlap cover and starts digging out the dirt doggy style. The small props and his evidence spill onto the floor cloth. Polygraph manipulates some of the little props as if they are blowing in the wind, whirling and twisting a sock, crashing and spinning cans and skidding the high heeled shoe through the dirt.

Polygraph places the trees, increasing the ferocity of his wind sounds. When he has placed the last tree, he picks up the dinner bell and rings it.

Music cue #1: Romantic, cheesy Russian love song.

Polygraph takes the white toy dogs in pairs and makes them float, dance, spin, copulate, howl with delight, and grub for food. Then he places the dogs in the dirt so they are all facing the suitcase.

Polygraph claps his hands to get the dogs' attention, then switches on the starlight backdrop in the suitcase.

Polygraph digs out the umbrella and places it on top of the opened suitcase. He digs out the red bone and floats it into position, crowning the umbrella. Then he singles out one dog—the lonely one—which he grabs and places on the suitcase above the others. It howls.

Arooooo-ooo

The other dogs howl in response.

Arooo-ooooo

Polygraph turns all the switches off, then turns directly to audience.

Polygraph: Just like that.

The lights snap to full.

"Have you ever taken an old prune and when you squish it, it makes a face just like this?"

Scene 5. Documents (flashback)

>*Polygraph trots over to the "office."*
>
>*The lights cross-fade to a harsh bright light which cuts sharply across the floor cloth downstage right.*
>
>*Polygraph stops to straighten his tie.*

Polygraph: I went to see him. I always went to see him in his office.

>*Polygraph knocks on the "door" (by stomping his foot).*

"Doctor": *(In German.)* Gesloten.

Polygraph: I translate: "Enter."

>He is there, always there, making those black marks in that blue book, and staring at those glass bottles on the wall, with things floating inside... I don't know why... I try to catch his eye.
>
>*Polygraph makes exaggerated movements to get the "Doctor's" attention. When the "Doctor" refuses to notice him, he blurts out—*
>
>I say: I need to have documents... He stands up. His eyes are hard... He says—

"Doctor": *(Looking disdainfully down at Polygraph.)* Where did you get that piece of trash hanging around your neck?

>*Polygraph looks up at him in surprise.*

Polygraph: My tie? My tie, I bought it on Kuznetsky bridge. All the girls really like that tie.

"Doctor": And those ridiculous shoes.

Polygraph: These are patent leather. Everyone wears patent leather.

"Doctor": Stop eating sunflower seeds in the apartment!

Polygraph: Okay. Okay.

"Doctor": Take care when you use the toilet!

Polygraph: Fine, fine…

"Doctor": Did you *kill* Mrs. Poliakoff's cat?

Polygraph: No way. She hit me first. I told her it was not *her* jaw to slap. It belongs to the government.

> *Pause.*
>
> *Polygraph changes his tone, desperately hoping the "Doctor" will listen to his appeal.*

I need to have documents. A man is strictly forbidden to exist without documents.

"Doctor": You do not need to have documents. You do not have a name!

Polygraph: A name, a name, everybody has a name. Once upon a time there was a little dog. He had a name. Everybody called him "Hey, You." You see? Even *You* is a name!

> *When Polygraph realizes that the "Doctor" is unmoved by his pleas, he turns and bursts out of the office.*
>
> *The lights brighten in centre area.*
>
> *Polygraph appeals directly to the audience.*

You see what that bastard can do? Son of a bitch. A name, a name…

Then I saw a calendar at the end of the hall. I took it. Many beautiful pictures.

> *Polygraph sits on the large suitcase and pretends to look at a "calendar."*

I am looking at it.

> *He leafs through the "calendar," looking for a name.*

This one... No, too many trees.

This one: Two boys playing with a ball outside of a school. No.

This one: A sailor leaning on the rail of a boat. Nope.

This one! A beautiful shining machine, with those black marks...

> *Polygraph leaps to his feet and trots downstage centre.*

I go to see my friends...they like me...*they* call me comrade.

> *He strikes his proud poses, nose in the air.*

I show them the calendar, the shining machine with those black marks, and they tell me my name very slowly... laughing.

> *He returns to the "office." The lights cross-fade. He knocks and enters, then tries in vain to catch the eye of the "Doctor."*

> *Polygraph rams his crumpled cigarette into his mouth.*

I have found myself a name...

> *Polygraph gets no reaction from the "Doctor." Nonetheless, he strikes a triumphant pose, nose in the air.*

My name is Polygraph Polygraphovich Sharikov...

> *Polygraph glances over at the "Doctor." He is puzzled by the "Doctor's" reaction.*

His eyes, they were...funny. His face...

> *Polygraph speaks directly to audience.*

Have you ever taken an old prune, and when you squish it, it makes a face just like this?

He gestures squishing a prune between his palms while he imitates the "Doctor's" grimace.

It was like that…with that old bastard… He started to laugh.

"Doctor": *(Sarcastically.)* Polygraph Polygraphovich Sharikov. Very interesting name.

Polygraph exits the office, and the lights cross-fade to centre lights. He paces as if walking with the "Doctor" in the "apartment hallway."

Polygraph: We go into the hall.

"Doctor": And where did you get such a name?

Polygraph: Oh, here in the apartment.

"Doctor": Where exactly?

Polygraph: Oh, hee-ere.

He put his arm around me. *(Softly.)* He was very warm. *(Polygraph laughs.)* I put my arm around him. He said—

"Doctor": And where precisely did you get such a name?

Polygraph: The wall.

"Doctor": The wall? How interesting.

Polygraph: It was a calendar.

"Doctor": A calendar? How very interesting. May I take a look at it?

Polygraph: Yes, of course. I have it with me right now.

Polygraph shows him the "calendar."

He took it. He was looking at it.

Polygraph watches the "Doctor" flip through the

"*calendar.*"

No, not that one, too many trees. No, not the two boys. Not the sailor leaning on the… This one, the beautiful shining machine, with those black marks…that is my name.

"Doctor": Polygraph Polygraphovich Sharikov. Very interesting name…

Polygraph: He went into that room…

Polgraph watches the "Doctor" move upstage right.

…the one with the smell of roast beef, and the things that go tinkling, tinkling, tinkling. He went over to the fire… He threw the calendar into the fire.

Polygraph bolts upstage centre to the "fire." He poses, his back to the audience, cocking his head like a dog, not at all understanding.

All those beautiful black marks, burning, turning into smoke.

Polygraph growls and gnashes his teeth. He bares his teeth and points at them. He races to the dirt pile in front of the dream suitcase. He digs out a piece of evidence—a charred piece of the calendar.

You see? I saved a piece… Polygraph Polygraphovich Sharikov…very interesting name.

He can barely contain his rage.

I will get my justice…

He shoves the scrap of calendar into his shirt pocket.

"I will protect that man, and my piece of sausage."

Scene 6. Story of a Man, a Piece of Sausage and a Dog.

The lights cross-fade to the intimate "storytelling" light. Polygraph crosses downstage centre, takes an agitated pull on his cigarette, then turns to the audience.

Polygraph: I tell you a story, the story of a man…a piece of sausage, and…a dog. Now, once upon a time there was a dog dying in the streets of Moscow. Now, that dog saw a bright light, and in that bright light, he saw a man walking. He came closer and closer and closer. He stood very still, like a tree frozen in Siberia. Now, that dog crawled out of the gateway to beside that man. He howled.

Aroooo-oooo

A shaft of bright white light cuts across downstage centre. Polygraph gazes up into the light. He poses tragically, remembering the ecstasy of smells. His voice is very fragile.

The smell rejuvenated me, lifted me from my belly—contracted for two days with fiery spasms. The heavenly smell of chopped horse meat mixed with garlic and pepper…

He stands over me. I can sense, I know, the sausage is in the right-hand pocket of his overcoat.

Glance at me… I am dying. We have the souls of slaves…and a wretched fate.

Arooooooooo

Just like that.

The lights cross-fade to the intimate "storytelling" light.

Now, that man reached into the pocket of his overcoat and broke off a piece of sausage. He tossed it into the air.

Now, that little dog thought, "I will show him my greatest talent."

He leaps to catch the "sausage."

Just like that. Now, that man said—

"Doctor": Come, *Sharik*.

Polygraph: That dog was amazed. He had never been called a name before, and he followed that man.

Panting rapidly, he follows the "man" over to stage left, then circles back to centre stage.

Just like that. Now, on the way, that dog saw a cat. He thought, "I will show him my greatest talent. I will protect that man, and *my* piece of sausage."

He barks ferociously at the "cat."

Woooh, wooh, aroo, wooh… INSOLENT TRASH, GODDAMNED INSOLENT TRASH! And that cat ran up the gutters and hissed like an old hose pipe. Now, that dog could see that man was very impressed. He followed that man…all the way home.

Polygraph makes the sound of the wind, tosses some confetti up into the air and walks into the little confetti blizzard.

And the wind took all the tracks away.

The lights cross-fade to cool blue "dream" light.

Polygraph crosses to the site of the first dream, and whispers to the little white dogs in the dirt.

He scatters some more confetti snow. He pairs up the little dogs, laying his red sock over one of the pairs.

He speaks to the little dogs.

Stay close…

"I know who he is. He is a wizard, a magician,
a sorcerer out of a dog's fairy tale.

Scene 7. The Story of a Man, the Smell of Roast Beef, and a Dog

The lights snap back to the intimate "storytelling" light.

Polygraph: Now, once upon a time, there was a dog who followed a man home.

Polygraph trots downstage centre.

He waited outside the apartment. He heard that man say—

"Doctor": Come in, *Mister Sharik.*

Polygraph: Now, that dog was amazed. He had never been called *Mister* before, and so he entered…

Polygraph grovels and whimpers.

Just like that. He saw many things. There, a lamp with a beautiful pink lampshade, and all the things that go tinkling, tinkling, tinkling. Now, he heard that man say—

"Doctor": Come, Mister Sharik. Let's eat.

Polygraph: He followed that man to a room…with a large table. Covered with a white table cloth… On it, much food. Now that dog, he went straight under the table…

Polygraph kneels and sniffs excitedly at the underside of the "table."

Just like this. Here, the smell of roast beef, with pepper and gravy… Here, the smell of a sturgeon cooking with lemon juice and butter… Here, Swiss cheese sweating on a black plate, and all those bottles all reflecting that light going tinkling, tinkling, tinkling.

He makes stabbing gestures with a fork.

Now, that man he took his fork and he stabbed a tidbit of roast beef, and he tossed it into the air.

Polygraph points to the "piece of roast beef" in mid-air.

Now, that dog, he saw it out of the corner of his eye. He thought, "I will show him my greatest talent"—a little bit of blood on it, some pepper and gravy... On his tongue *(He shows his tongue.)* very excited...in his tummy...*(He points to his stomach.)*...a little battle going on...

Polygraph gestures to indicate the battle going on in his stomach among all the small hungry voices.

—Will he catch it?

—I don't know.

—Please, please, I'm very hungry.

—Me too, me too...

Polygraph leaps to gobble up the "piece of roast beef."

A shaft of bright white light cuts across the downstage area. Polygraph poses tragically, gazing up into the light, remembering the joy and happiness. His voice is fragile.

He is concerned about me. I know who he is. He is a wizard, a magician, a sorcerer out of a dog's fairy tale. But what if this is a dream? What if there is nothing? No warmth? No full stomach? No lamp with the beautiful pink lampshade? Again the cold, the snow, the vicious people, the cafeteria. Oh God, how bitter that will be...

Arooooo-ooooooo

Just like that.

The lights cross-fade to the "storytelling" light.

Now, that man bought that dog a beautiful collar and a leash, and the maid took him for a walk every day... Just like this.

Polygraph grabs his tie and pulls himself forward, imitating a dog being walked, straining at the leash.

At first he did not like it. He would see the other dogs and they would yell, "Hey you, six legs! Hey you, gentleman's scum!" But then he saw a fierce jealousy in those dogs' eyes.

Still on the "leash," Polygraph begins to strut proudly, crossing to centre stage, his nose in the air.

He thought, "I am a gentleman's dog. I have tasted a better life. And what is freedom anyway? A puff of smoke dreamt up by those democrats!" Now, that dog followed that maid home, and went straight under the table…

Polygraph watches the "dog" go under the table.

…where he was warm and fat and happy.

He speaks directly to the audience.

Have you ever thought that maybe you have died and gone to heaven?

He gazes heavenward and gives a little howl…

Arooooo

For that dog…it was just like that.

Polygraph takes a thoughtful drag on his cigarette.

Scene 8. At the Table (flashback)

Lights snap up on "dinner table" area.

"Doctor": Sit!

Polygraph races to sit on a suitcase stage right.

Polygraph: You see? I'm sitting.

"Doctor": Say hello!

Polygraph mutters oaths under his breath, then obediently raises a paw.

Polygraph: You see? I say hello.

"Doctor": Fetch!

Polygraph: *(Muttering under his breath.)* I don't fetch. Bastard, son of a bitch…

He capitulates after a moment, tosses his cigarette onto the floor, then fetches it.

You see? I'm fetching.

"Doctor": Don't smoke at the table.

Polygraph butts his cigarette on the floor.

Polygraph: I don't smoke at the table.

"Doctor": Eat!

Polygraph: A fork, a knife, I am eating…

He starts to eat.

"Doctor": Use a napkin when you eat.

Polygraph looks around for a napkin. Seeing none, he stuffs the end of his tie into his collar. He wolfs down some "food," and gulps down some "vodka." Then he speaks directly to the audience.

Polygraph: Good food here, very good food.

> *As he chomps on his food, he lifts an ear flap and cocks his head, listening and imitating the fragments of table conversation.*

Like that, they would be talking. Six eyes going back and forth across the table…talking, talking.

"Guest": Politics…Bolshoi Theatre…

> *Polygraph hiccups.*

"Guest": Politics, recognition of America…

Polygraph: *(Interrupting.)* I would say, "Hey you, give me a smoke or I give you a poke."

"Guest": Nuclear physics.

Polygraph: *(Rudely.)* Hey you, little apple.

"Guest": Rejuvenation is a possible thing in this day and age!

> *Lifting his glass in a toast, Polygraph interrupts again.*

Polygraph: Bourgeoisie!

Six eyes looking at me…then that bastard with the eyes at the back of his head says—

"Doctor": *(Exasperated.)* So, perhaps you should read a book?

Polygraph: I already read a book. *(Polygraph hiccups.)* He is amazed.

"Doctor": And *what* book, may I ask, have you read?

> *Polygraph stands and digs for his cigarettes.*

Polygraph: I stood up. I took out a cigarette.

> *Pause. He scratches himself.*

Yuh, unh, um, yeah… I dunno aroooo…

> *Pause.*

Correspondence! You know, that guy Kautsky was writing to this guy Engels... The table...it jumped six feet in the air... Six eyes staring at me...That bastard says—

"Doctor": And may I ask you, what is your opinion of *that* book?

Polygraph speaks directly to the audience.

Polygraph: My opinion, my opinion. He *asked* me...my opinion.

Pause.

Well, you take everything...

Polygraph gathers up all the "dinner dishes" on the "table," then redistributes them to the "guests."

...and divide it up!... Good, unh?

Polygraph looks to the "Doctor" for approval.

He comes closer and closer and closer...

Polygraph stiffens.

He stands very still, like a tree frozen in Siberia. I feel very cold and small.

"Doctor": It's MONSTROUS. IT'S MONSTROUS...

Polygraph: He looked right through me...to the back of my head, as if trying to peer at all my thoughts.

"Doctor": STAND!

Polygraph leaps to his feet.

Polygraph: You see? I'm standing.

"Doctor": You are the lowest rung of development. You are a creature just in the process of formation with a feeble intellect. All your actions are the actions of an animal. Yet you permit yourself to speak with utterly insufferable impudence, to a man with a university education…to offer advice on the cosmic scale, and of the equally cosmic stupidity, on how to divide everything up…right after you gobble down a whole boxful of tooth powder, too.

Polygraph wrenches his gaze away from the "Doctor."

Polygraph: His eyes went away for a moment… I could breathe.

He speaks directly to the audience.

You see what that bastard can do?

Polygraph eyes are pulled back to the "Doctor."

His eyes came back on fire…fixing me.

"Doctor": Try to learn. Try to become a more or less acceptable member of our society… Find yourself a position.

Breaking away again from the Doctor's gaze, Polygraph sneers.

Polygraph: A position. "Find yourself a position." Bastard, an animal, an animal… So what? I'm an animal.

Polygraph takes a nervous drag on his cigarette.

"I am a gentleman's dog. I have tasted a better life."

Scene 9. The Job (Flashback)

> *The lights cross-fade to create strong blue backlights which cast nocturnal shadows on the floor cloth.*

Polygraph: I got a job, a very good job. *They* gave me papers.

> *He bolts to the dirt pile and unearths his work papers.*

You see? It says…um, unh… I don't read too good…

> *Looking at the dirty torn documents, he tries to make out the words.*

The person who is holding these papers…(*He points at himself.*)…is permitted to work for the City of Moscow, to purge the city of stray animals…especially cats. Signed, the City of Moscow.

> *Polygraph stuffs the papers into his shirt pocket.*

They come for me at night…

> *He sits on the suitcase stage right and scratches himself absentmindedly, waiting.*

I hear a pebble touch the window.

> *Polygraph leaps into action, stealthily crossing to the downstage left corner of the floor cloth to look out the "window."*

I can see the truck waiting for me below…

> *He pads softly back to centre stage.*

They let me ride in the back.

> *Polygraph veers back to the large suitcase and sits, as if riding in the back of the truck. He laughs deliriously.*

We go. I don't know where… We go… They say stop. They say go.

Polygraph leaps from "the truck" and goes obediently.

You see? I am going...

He stares into the lights.

All I can see are the street lights. The people...they watch me very closely. They know who I am...

Polygraph points to the papers in his pocket. His eyes become slits.

Specialist.

He points to his goggles.

You see these goggles? They gave them to me to protect my eyes. It's a very dangerous job.

He pulls the goggles over his eyes and whirls around, hunting.

I see what I am looking for.

He moves swiftly and dangerously over to the dirt pile.

I go closer and closer and closer... I stand very still, like a tree frozen in Siberia.

Polygraph stiffens, then stands very still.

Silence.

He speaks softly, menacingly.

Here Kitty, Kitty, Kitty... Hee-ere Kitty, Kitty.

Snatching up a "cat," Polygraph strokes it while speaking Russian-sounding gibberish.

I translate: "Nice cat."

He grabs the "cat" by the neck.

Insolent trash.

Polygraph turns his attention back to the audience.

Now, for those of you who are squeamish, it is best to turn your eyes...

He spins around and strangles the "cat," then turns back to face the audience.

It's a good job. They pay me well.

Lights snap up in "office" area.

Polygraph looks towards the "office." He straightens his tie, crossing over to the "door." He knocks and barges in.

He is there, always there, making those black marks in that blue book, and staring at those glass bottles on the wall... I don't know why... I try to catch his eye.

Polygraph tries to get the Doctor's attention. When the "Doctor" finally looks up, Polygraph strikes his arrogant pose, puffing on his cigarette.

I have found myself a position... He stands up fast, his eyes are white.

"Doctor": You smell of *cat urine.*

Polygraph: Naturally. It's the position.

"Doctor": And what do you do?

Polygraph: Yesterday we choked them and choked them and choked them.

"Doctor": Then what?

Polygraph: I dunno...unh, um. They make them into squirrel coats and they sell them to the workers...for credit.

Polygraph bursts out of the "office."

He chased me into the hall, he grabbed my tie, and twisted it...

Polygraph yanks his tie up, dangling on the end of it as if it is being twisted by the "Doctor."

He speaks directly to the audience.

Look at that! Do you see what that bastard did to me?

Polygraph chokes as he speaks.

"Doctor": I forbid you to have that stinking job.

Abruptly released from the tie, Polygraph points offstage.

Polygraph: You see? He is *dangerous*.

"*Yesterday we choked them and choked them and choked them.*"

Scene 10. The Story of the Bright Light, the Smell of Death and a Dog

Polygraph takes a moment to collect himself. He takes a few ragged puffs on his cigarette. Still agitated, he turns to face the audience.

The lights change to the intimate "storytelling" light.

Polygraph: I tell you a story. The story of a bright light, the smell of death, and…a dog.

Now, once upon a time, there was a dog who was fat and warm and happy. Now, that man, he took that dog and he locked him in the toilet. That dog howled…

Aroooo

Just like that. And he scratched…

Polygraph scratches himself.

Just like that. Now that man came, and he took that dog by the collar, and he led him to a room that he had never seen before. It was all white.

Now, that man, he took that dog and he put him on a table. Not a table for eating. Now, that dog, he smelled something worse than dead cats…

He followed that smell, to where he saw beside him…a long package. Covered with a white cloth, with two feet sticking out. And on one toe, a little white ticket. Now, that dog looked away, and all he could see were six eyes dressed in white, staring at him…

A bright spotlight snaps up on Polygraph. He stares into it.

Then a bright light was switched on, fixing his eyes.

He pulls his gaze away from the light and speaks, directly, intimately to the audience.

Have you ever stared into a bright light, and then when you look away, all you can see are little white lights? For that dog it was just like that.

Now, that man, he took a white cloth, and he dipped it in green liquid, and he held it over the face of that dog. Now that little dog breathed in.

Polygraph takes a surprised breath.

He thought…

He speaks to the bright light, his voice very fragile.

Brothers, murderers, why do you do this to me? Thank you very much. It's been a wonderful life. I don't know what I would have done without you. Good bye, Moscow. I'm off to Paradise for my long patience in this dog's life…

Polygraph turns back to the audience.

Now, his eyes rolled to the back of his head, and he had a dream… Just like this…

The Dream of Paradise

Scene 11. The Dream of Paradise

Polygraph crawls on all fours upstage right to the second suitcase. In the suitcase are all the materials to create the second dream installation. There is a pillow with fibre-fill stuffing. Beneath the pillow is the "machine," which is a collapsible kinetic sculpture. The centre wheel of the sculpture has six spokes which support small "Chagallesque" dogs made of papier mâché. These spin around the axis, powered by a small electric motor and drive belts.

In the base of the sculpture is a car cassette player and speaker, various wires, and control switches. Also stored in the suitcase are toy dog angels, all with halos, as well as a small travelling cloud and the battery.

Polygraph manipulates all the objects, the machine, the travelling cloud and the cassette.

The lighting is high angle reds and yellows with low foot lights to create a hallucinatory effect.

Dream installation:

Polygraph careens to the suitcase, laughing and half mad. He goes down on his hands and knees to open the suitcase. Opening it, he sighs and rests his head on the pillow for a moment. He switches on the music.

Music cue #2: Acid Russian rock music screams from the suitcase.

Polygraph grabs the pillow and slowly pulls the fibre-fill stuffing out. He creates clouds with the stuffing, and plays with them in the red and yellow light. Then he places the clouds in front of the machine. He takes the small angel dogs, making them fly and cavort, before setting them down gently in the fibre-fill clouds.

He carefully opens out the mechanical sculpture to its operating position. He disengages the wires and the spokes, and sets the papier mâché dogs on the ferris wheel.

He takes the little travelling cloud out of the suitcase and floats it to the Dream of the Parkl installation on stage left.

The lights fade up to cool blue "dream" light.

Polygraph brings the cloud down to land near the lonely little dog that has been left on the suitcase. He grabs the lonely dog and smashes it in the dirt in front of the other white toy dogs. The dogs howl in agony.

Arooooo oooo oooooo

Polygraph retrieve sthe travelling cloud, then floats it over to pick up the "dead" lonely dog. He takes up the travelling cloud with the dead dog now on it and crosses back to the machine. He turns on the little halo light in the travelling cloud..

Polygraph howls in pain.

Polygraph: Arooooooo-ooo

He places the dog and travelling cloud in front of the fibre-fill clouds. He brings out other angel dogs to comfort the dead lonely one.

He switches on the machine. The ferris wheel spins precariously. Floor lighting creates eerie shadows.

Over the sound of the music, Polygraph cries out to the other toy dogs in the dirt.

You see that? You see what that bastard did to me?

Sputtering and cursing, he laps up some water, then crawls back to the suitcase.

Green eyes...she was beautiful... I'll get my justice.

Polygraph switches off the music, lights, and machine. He turns to the audience and gestures to the dream installation.

Just like that...

Scene 12: Rumours

> *Lights snap to full brightness.*
>
> *Polygraph careens downstage centre, and begins to imitate the fragments of gossip he has heard on the street below the "apartment."*

"Gossip": Have you heard? A crazy man living in Obukhov lane.

"Gossip": Oh no…really?

"Gossip": I have heard that there is a huge monster living there.

"Gossip": Really?

"Gossip": It is a baby monster living there!

"Gossip": Oh, no… Really?

"Gossip": I have heard that it is a baby who plays the violin!

"Gossip": Really?… No.

"Gossip": Oh yes, and I have heard that it is a baby born to a woman who cannot have children!

> *Polygraph lets out a crazy laugh. He is appalled at the gossips' stupidity, but also proud that people are talking about him.*

Polygraph: I could hear them outside the apartment, down by the potato sellers. Talking…talking. Many people standing there, and pointing. A man with green hair…a woman covered with red splotches. Old people, all shouting:

"Crowd": REJUVENATE ME, REJUVENATE ME!

> *Polygraph cocks an ear sharply as he catches an interesting snippet from the street below.*

Gossips: I hear, "It is a miracle… It came from the sky… It is a Martian…and… IT IS ANNOUNCING THE END OF THE WORLD IN TWENTY-TWO DAYS!"

> *Polygraph laughs insanely, and goes to lean at "window" downstage left.*

Polygraph: I say, "HEY YOU."

> *He yells at the gossipmongers down in the street below the "window."*

"END OF THE WORLD IN TWENTY-TWO DAYS!"

THE STREETS WENT BERSERK!

> *Polygraph laughs uproariously and stumbles around the space chaotically, drunk with his power.*
>
> *The telephone rings.*

Dring Dring... Dring Dring...Dring...

> *He makes a move to answer the phone, speaking offhandedly.*

Telephone... I get it.

"Doctor": *(Putting a stop to the ruckus.)* HANDS OFF THAT PHONE.

> *Polygraph speaks directly to the audience.*

Polygraph: That bastard was sitting there with another pair of eyes...reading the paper.

> *He dives into the dirt pile to unearth some crumpled newspaper.*

Just like this. He said—

"Doctor": *(Reading aloud in a sarcastic tone.)* Listen to this...seven people arrested for spreading a rumour that a Martian is living in Obukhov lane...and because of that event, the End of the World is predicted in twenty-two days... *(He laughs sardonically.)* Idiots. They will believe anything.

Polygraph: Then those eyes turned to *me*...laughing. My tie, I bought it on Kuznetsky...my shoes, they are patent leather... Then, that bastard, he took that paper and he *ripped* it, and he made it into a small ball...

Polygraph balls up the newspaper.

Just like that. And he tossed it over his shoulder towards the fire.

He draws a large arc in the air with the balled-up newspaper.

I saw it out of the corner of my eye, all those beautiful black marks turning.

He snatches the newspaper out of the air, dashes to stage centre, and speaks directly to the audience.

I caught it... You see that? I will get my justice...

Polygraph stuffs the paper into his shirt pocket. He strikes an arrogant pose, nose in the air. He struts across the floor cloth, sucking on a filthy cigarette.

I am a handsome devil. I am perhaps an unknown prince.

He stops, his voice becoming uncertain.

It is very possible that my grandmother sinned with a Newfoundland...Where does this white spot on my chin come from, I ask you?

His confidence is completely shaken.

He is a man with excellent taste. He just wouldn't pick up any stray mutt.

Scene 13. The Girl Reprise (flashback)

The lights intensify a few degrees.

Polygraph careens around the stage, fragments of remembered events pouring out in a stream of consciousness.

Polygraph: She likes me. I say to her, "I'm a good man. I have a good psyche. It's just cats I hate." She wants to see my apartment. I show her the lamp with the beautiful pink lampshade, and all the things that go tinkling, tinkling, tinkling. I can see in her green eyes that she is impressed by my apartment.

Outside "office" area, he stops and listens.

All I can hear is crying, crying, crying…

"Doctor": Here is twenty-five chervontsy. You'd better stay away from him. He is no good for nothing.

Polgraph slowly backs away from the "office door."

Polygraph: I see that spit coming toward me out of the corner of my eye. It is bitter, covered with blood and lemon juice… On each little gob, I can see knives and razor blades churning.

The "spit" hits Polygraph on the cheek, and he crumples to the floor whimpering.

Suddenly, he explodes in a fierce howl.

Aroooooooo-Ooooo Oooooo

Polygraph veers over to the dirt pile. He scratches in the dirt and digs out a small revolver.

He shows the gun to the audience.

Look at this…look, look at this…

Polygraph crosses to "office," knocks once, then crashes through the door. He points the gun at the "Doctor."

Right between the eyes.

Polygraph laughs insolently.

He stands up... His eyes go from white to black to red.

Polygraph waves the gun, taunting the "Doctor."

Hey, give me a smoke or I give you a poke. Evening Paper.

His voice becomes bitter.

Hey you, little apple.

He gives the "Doctor" a disdainful look.

Bourgeoisie.

For the first time he had nothing to say.

Pause.

His eyes, they were funny... They moved from side to side.

Polygraph looks over his shoulder and is shocked by what he sees there.

There was a man standing behind me!

Polygraph drops to his knees as if struck on the back of the head. He appeals directly to the audience.

He hit me. He hit me with that pillow I had so many beautiful dreams on.

Still on his knees, Polygraph crawls across the floor as if he is being restrained by the leg and held in an arm lock.

He pleads with the audience.

You see that? Look. Look what he did to me. He took me by the leg...and look, the arm...like that. I'll get my justice. Look at that.

Polygraph struggles to his feet, and looks at the "Doctor."

Then he said something... He did not even look at me. He was looking at his fingers.

Polygraph examines his nails, then raises his index finger.

I think it was that one.

"Doctor": *(Calm and controlled.)* You have fifteen minutes to pack everything, pack your trousers...all... AND GET OUT OF THIS APARTMENT.

Polygraph backs away, sputtering.

Polygraph: You bast... This...sixteen square arsh... I'll get my just... Son of a bitch...

Polygraph is thrown onto the street. He lands hard. He spits poisonously, and points offstage.

He is dangerous.

"There was a man standing behind me!"

Scene 14. Story of the End of the World

Lights cross-fade to make eerie shadows.

Polygraph: I tell you one more story. The story of a man, a blue book and…a dog. Now, once upon a time, there was a man who wrote many things in a blue book.

Polygraph dashes to the dirt pile and unearths the blue book. He starts flipping through the book.

Just like this…

He speaks intimately to the audience.

I don't read too good.

January 5th… Found…dog.

Polygraph scratches and lets out a confused little howl.

Arooo

January 10th… Dog…fat…warm…happy.

January 25th… Dead body…four hours old… Operation success.

Polygraph whimpers.

February 5th… It walks…it talks…give me a smoke or I give you a poke.

Polygraph's voice almost breaks.

Hey you, little apple…

He closes the book.

Silence.

End of the world…fifteen minutes…

Waving the book, Polygraph laughs insanely.

I WILL GET MY JUSTICE.

> *Polygraph prepares for the "End of the World." He places all his evidence that is stuffed into his shirt pocket on the canvas floor cloth. He pulls wires from the large suitcase and attaches them to the samovar. He pulls wires and switches from the smaller suitcase as well.*

> *While he prepares, Polygraph mutters ominously.*

She was beautiful...high heeled shoes...he was warm, fat, happy...a tidbit of roast beef...tinkling, tinkling, tinkling...it's a good job...

> *Polygraph grabs a small mechanical dog from the large suitcase. He struggles with some wires, then sticks them into the head and tail of the mechanical dog. He laughs. He turns on all the lights in the dream sets.*

> *He finds a little switch and flicks it. The ratty umbrella turns crazily.*

> *Music cue #3: Loud and angry Russian rock and roll.*

> *Polygraph flicks on all the other switches. The samovar agitates chaotically, the mechanical dog marches and falls, and the ferris wheel machine spins out of control...*

> *Polygraph surveys the scene, then calmly lights a cigarette. He gazes heavenward expectantly.*

> *Pause.*

> *Polygraph ignites the samovar. Smoke explodes from it.*

> *Polygraph is triumphant.*

I WILL GET MY JUSTICE!

> *The music increases in intensity...*

> > *Blackout.*

"I will get my justice!"

Writer/Director's Notes

When I agreed to read Mikhail Bulgakov's novella *Heart of a Dog* with an eye to adapting it for the stage, I had no idea the kind of adventure Robert Astle and I were embarking on, and no way of knowing all the personal and artistic discoveries he and I would make.

From that first reading, I was profoundly moved, both by the story itself and by the concerns it dealt with. I wondered how we could ever convey the power of this book without betraying its spirit. How could we manage to show the relationship between the individual and the state and all the complexity of characters and ideas while still remaining true to the author?

Through mockery, tragedy, comedy, metaphor?

Through theatre which directly engages the public? Certainly.

In poetic form? Cruel, perhaps.

Robert already had a fairly clear idea of what he wanted, and he quickly proposed a detailed adaptation of the novella, a solo work.

I do not believe in "directing" or "producing" actors, and would rather discover in their depths what moves them on stage. In this way I am able to collaborate in the creative process instead of imposing the traditional power relationship between director and actor.

I agreed to take on the project on condition that Robert and I would begin by forgetting everything we thought we knew about the piece, working the text and story as sculptors might, allowing ourselves to jumble everything up, turn it every which way, and look at it from many different angles. I wanted to avoid a logical adaptation that wouldn't allow us to discover ourselves through the story. I wanted us to let ourselves be surprised by the vivid details and then to push those details as far as they would go, taking us step by step towards our goal.

As we were beginning work on the piece, the walls around the Eastern bloc countries were beginning to come down, revealing a multitude of lost and destitute individuals. This kept us aware of our own time and its daily realities; this guided us in our choices.

I believe that both work and thought in theatre happen first and foremost in the playing space, that the truth is found *on* the stage. Outside this space our thoughts continue, but our most beautiful, our most inspired ideas are worthless unless they are tested. I wanted to start immediately, working our thoughts and ideas out physically in the rehearsal studio.

We worked in our tiny studio in Rhodes-Saint-Genese, face to face every day, both of us in a state of heightened alertness.

There was a story to tell, but where to begin? There was Robert who wanted to tell this story, but why? There were all our desires and all the images overwhelming us.

We began with the story. First, sitting like a storyteller by the fire, Robert recounted it. Then he improvised on the story, again and again, exploding all over the studio space as he played one character after another, without using a single prop.

A whole variety of events and situations and throng of characters were jostling for room on the stage. Things were starting to get crowded. We had to find a motor. We were in danger of losing sight of the original intent, of losing the power of the novella. We were drowning in an accumulation of little stories that had to be told if we were to hold onto the coherence of the piece. This whole work period enabled us to break up the story into different scenes, to concentrate on those stories that we found particularly powerful and progressive. This was enjoyable, but what did we really want to accomplish? We often asked ourselves this question.

During this process it seemed important to me that both Robert and I present a weekly synthesis of our research, a kind of public confrontation, which would allow us to identify where we were, what juncture we had reached in our thinking. I proposed a series of "Thursday Night Meetings," which several friends attended, including Didier Caffonnette who would become our production designer. These meetings were always rich, positive and rewarding experiences that allowed us to make the point and carry on.

Next, we tried telling the story using props, objects and toys.

Often Robert left early in the morning before rehearsals. He walked the streets and scoured the flea markets, seeking out faces, attitudes, expressions, objects, clothes, chance encounters. He always returned enchanted, always with fresh material to inspire us.

As a storyteller, playing all the different characters, who was Robert really? For him to tell the story this way required many props and little puppets. But when Robert manipulated the small plush dog, Little Sharik, who was he? The doctor? A character—The Manipulator—outside the story? Or was he Polygraph? If so, should Polygraph manipulate the little figure of himself beforehand, or should we first show his soul?

Then Robert took on the actual character of the dog. The howling, the barking, the running, the yelping of Sharik echoed all through the neighbourhood. Looking at this actor as he played the dog, with his half-dog, half-man appearance and expressions and all his vulgarity (and I use the term here in the sense of buffoonery), I said to myself, "Here is our motor."

Here was the man with the heart of a dog, the unfortunate creature, the bastard. Here was the crude, revolting man, claiming his turf, scurrilous and insulting. Here was the little being looking up imploringly at the world, at his master.

So, another phase began. The meaning of the piece was no longer obscure. At this point, I needed to identify the truly poignant moments in the actor's performance and develop the character with these details, these concrete building blocks on which he could lean. Sometimes, however, Polygraph and I simply had to wait while the actor found the best in himself.

And so, with much trial and error, with many doubts and revelations, with much joy and trepidation, we pushed forward to the finished production.

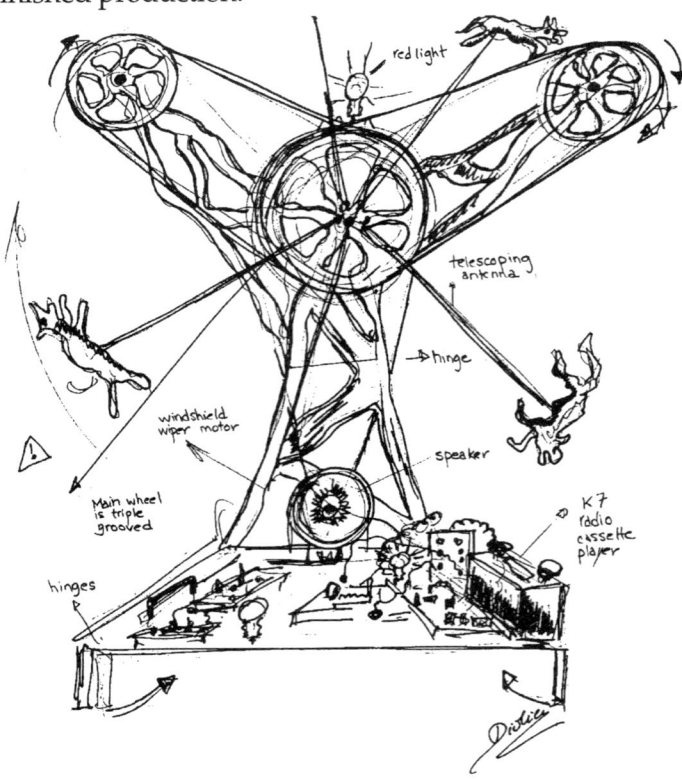

Writer/Performer's Notes

When we began working on *Heart of A Dog*, I had just finished ten years of working with Small Change Theatre, an Alberta-based clown and mask theatre collective, and I was at the point in my career when I needed to make some substantial changes in my creative process if I was to continue working in the theatre. I gave myself these directives: One, development time, so that I could explore building a solo theatre performance piece outside of a company format. Two, to create a work that had resonance. Three, to find the right collaborator.

Solo theatre expression has always appealed to me. The shows I liked best always featured a strong rapport with the audience—the shared space. I also liked the fact that the actor had to draw upon on all the essentials of performance dynamics: generosity, physicality, and virtuosity. I had seen some wonderful work, and found it very inspiring—Boleslav Polivka, and Joseph van De Berg, comic actors who played buffoons and clowns, but at the core of their work were communicating something very human and alive.

Finding a collaborator who can work with ideas, start from scratch, and bring a critical eye to a project is not an easy task. After ten years of collective work I had developed a very specific perspective. What I was looking for in a collaborator was someone who had a deep understanding of process and a willingness to really push at the right moment.

When I saw Agnès Limbos perform her solo show *Little Pea*, at the Edmonton Children's Festival in the late 1980's, I was totally bedazzled by the visual magic, Agnès' generosity, and her rapport with the audience. But even more important, what she had to say was both complex and delightful. I asked her if she would be interested in developing a solo work with me. She suggested I contact her when I had a concrete proposal.

I had been playing with the idea of doing a show from the point of view of a dog. I looked at texts, political cartoons, dog behavior books, even dog movies, but found nothing very compelling. I knew I didn't want to crawl around on all fours, and howl like some fun-fur clad idiot. I wanted to combine some of the physicality and "monstrousness" of Buffoon Theatre, which I had developed during a workshop with Serge Martin in 1987, with a dog's uncanny perception of human kind.

In 1988, while visiting my Russian friends Marina Popova and Alex Nadezdhin in Montreal, I told them about the dog project I was thinking about. They were suprised I had not heard about Bulgakov, and insisted I read *Heart of a Dog*. I read the book, at first in a kind of wired numbness, shocked by the ferocity, the theatricality, and the stinging black humor.

I wrote to Agnès to tell her of my discovery, and to the publisher asking for the rights. At the publisher's request, I went to New York to meet with the translator, Mirra Ginsburg. I explained my project to her in detail. She was doubtful—an unknown Canadian actor lands on her doorstep with a view to taking on a Russian novella by an author the stature of Bulgakov? And all from the point of view of the dog! But she said yes. Mirra's agreement was the turning point for this project, and her knowledge and understanding of Russian literature, poetry, folk tales, and writers has been an enormous inspiration to my creative life.

In 1989, the project was given wheels via a Canada Council Project Grant. In the summer of 1990, I finally arrived at Agnès' studio in Belgium, after three years of researching, negotiating for the rights, and wrapping up Small Change Theatre. The five-month rehearsal period that followed was one of the most rich and vivid periods in my life. Our collaboration was always intense, creative, and detailed. We became inoculated with each other's work. In November 1990, we previewed the show in our studio with success. My rehearsal notes read: "What a collaboration. The piece is good. Now, to search for audiences. Who will want this 'dog show' in their life?"

During this five-month process of creation, the text was always being generated, through improvisations, and what we called working "at the table"—analyzing the novella, discussing the work, and making notes. Only in the last phase, when we were really setting the structure and what needed to be said, did we focus on writing out the text.

When the offer came to publish this work, we turned back to our raw kitchen table script, which had been distilled from hundreds of hours of improvising, taping and transcribing, and to date, more than seventy performances in Canada, Belgium, the UK and the USA. So now—for the moment—it is caught on the page.

Notes on the Adaptation

The initial impulse for this project was to create a show from the dog's point of view. We chose to build the work as a solo piece, which both limited us and opened new horizons. Readers who know Bulgakov's novella will see immediately that this adaptation is not literal. We wanted our mongrel adaptation to reflect Bulgakov's ferocity, concise language, searing black humour, and visual poetry. The essence of this collaboration, and the adaptation that came out of it, was to keep the integrity and the spirit of the author's writing. If we offend, we offend, but if we surprise, then we have done our job.

For this work, we focussed on a moment from near the end of the book, when Polygraph is faced with the threat of being thrown onto the streets. That moment is our initiating force. Polygraph is propelled into the street, where he recounts in flashback and storytelling fashion the things that have happened to him. As he says: *You would not believe what he did to me.*

Notes on Performance

The central character in the play is inspired by Polygraph Polygraphovich Sharikov, the vulgar dog-man who is the result of an operation—the double transplant of the testes and pituitary gland from a dead criminal—on the stray dog Sharik.

Polygraph is man-made, like his literary cousin, Frankenstein. He has very little history. Is he a monster? Perhaps. A nightmare? Absolutely. He has his instincts (he hates cats), but can read Engels. His heart is torn between that of a man (albeit a petty criminal), and that of a dog. He is alone, looking for justice. The comic and tragic potential is rich. Polygraph is the sum of what was implanted in him, and what he learns to survive. His needs are simple: documents to give him an identity, a job, a place to live, a girl.

This work is a challenge for an actor. But why not? Any solo work is. Definitely, it is a role for an actor who loves transitions, ruptures of logic and coherence, contact with the audience, an actor who understands derision and physical expression, and is a keen observer of dog behavior.

Notes on Design

For the designer, this work poses many particular problems, so we have included the descriptions of the objects and the dream sequences, as well as drawings from the designer and "machiniste" Didier Caffonnette. Visually we were very inspired by L'Art Brut or Outsider Art. The colours and the movement of the dogs are inspired by Chagall. The mechanical machine, whirling umbrella, and agitating samovar are not props in the conventional sense; they are all found objects necessary for Polygraph's quest, visual and metaphorical proof of justice. At the end of the play *tout bouge!*

For this book, I would like to thank Agnès, who kept watch by her fax machine in Belgium, my editor Karen Haughian, who put up with my howling and scratching, and Mirra Ginsburg, Billy Merwick, and Harry Standjofski for corrections and notes. I would also like to thank my partner, mate and "fellow traveller" Trish Barclay, who inspires me with her great Northern spirit, and my son Simon, who was with me in Belgium at the very beginning, and one day will read this play.

Robert Astle

Robert Astle is an Albertan by birth. In 1978 he went to Paris to study theatre, improvisation acrobatics and creation at the famed Ecole Jacques Lecoq. It was there that he first met Agnès Limbos. In 1982, he co-founded Small Change Theatre, an Edmonton theatre collective, co-creating, producing and performing in its internationally acclaimed clown and mask shows *Hazard And Darlene In Love*, *At The Beach*, and *One Beautiful Evening* which toured to festivals and theatres in England, Scotland, France, New Zealand, Australia, Singapore, Japan, the United States, and Canada. In 1990, Astle returned to Europe to collaborate on the creation of his one-man show *Heart of a Dog* with Agnès Limbos, which has toured to festivals and theatres in Belgium, Canada, the United Kingdom, and the United States. Astle currently resides in the Yukon Territory. He divides his time between the North of 60 and Belgium, directing, teaching, writing, and performing.

Agnès Limbos

Passionate about theatre from a young age, Limbos began a career in theatre in her home city of Brussels, Belgium. After studying at Ecole Jacques Lecoq, she embarked on a path of international theatre collaboration and creation. In 1984 she created La Compagnie Gare Centrale, which has been garnering worldwide acclaim ever since. She has performed her astounding "Object Theatre" shows *Petrouchka*, *Petit Pois*, *Le Grand Malheur*, and *Le Sourire du Fou* in Germany, Spain, England, France, Hong Kong, the United States, and Canada.

Didier Caffonnette

Designer, builder, sculptor, "machiniste," technician, actor, and stuntman, Caffonnette brings an extraordinary talent to the theatre. He created the amazing machines and moving objects for La Compagnie Gare Centrale's production of *Petit Pois* and *Le Sourire du Fou*. For *Heart of a Dog*, Caffonnette built a whirling, spinning, sculptural backdrop, working with windshield wiper motors, batteries of all sizes, small electronics, wood, papier mâché, and found objects. He was inspired by the bizarre and wonderful expression called L'Art Brut. In 1983 he created his own street show *Le Train d'Enfer* and has performed it at summer festivals across Belgium.

Mikhail Bulgakov

Mikhail Bulgakov was born in Kiev in 1891. He practised medicine for a number of years, but gave up this career for writing. Bulgakov's work was under constant attack by Communist Party critics, who nonetheless refused his requests to emigrate after the Russian Revolution. Bulgakov's plays enjoyed popular success for a time, however, particularly *The Days of the Turbins*, *Zoyka's Apartment*, and *The Purple Island*. But by the 1930s, Bulgakov's work could no longer be published in his own country. His masterpiece, *The Master and Margarita*, was written in secrecy during the last years of his life. In 1940, after years of censorship, and the constant fear of being "removed" by the authorities, Bulgakov died of kidney disease.

It was not until the 1980s, with glasnost, that Bulgakov was "rehabilitated" and his work finally published in Russia. Since then his novels, plays and short stories have been published and produced internationally. Bulgakov is now considered to be one of the literary giants of the post-revolutionary period.